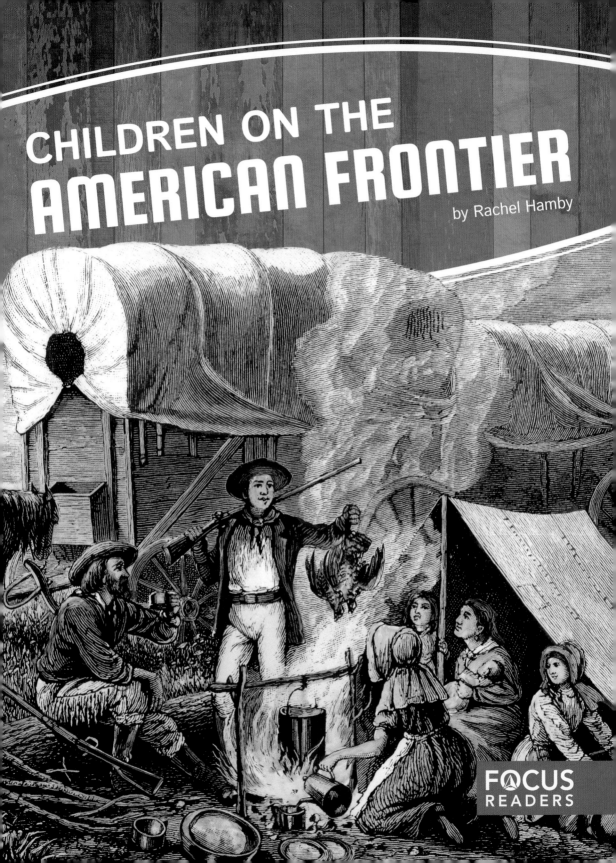

CHILDREN ON THE AMERICAN FRONTIER

by Rachel Hamby

FOCUS
READERS

www.focusreaders.com

Copyright © 2019 by Focus Readers, Lake Elmo, MN 55042. All rights reserved. No part of this book may be reproduced or utilized in any form or by any means without written permission from the publisher.

Focus Readers is distributed by North Star Editions:
sales@northstareditions.com | 888-417-0195

Produced for Focus Readers by Red Line Editorial.

Content Consultant: Yoav Hamdani, PhD Candidate, Department of History, Columbia University

Photographs ©: North Wind Picture Archives, cover, 1, 4–5, 6, 28–29, 35, 42–43, 45; Edward S. Curtis/Edward S. Curtis Collection/Library of Congress, 8–9, 12, 41; Orlando Scott Goff/Library of Congress, 11; Library of Congress/Corbis Historical/Getty Images, 15; Kansas State Historical Society, 16–17; MoniqueRodriguez/iStockphoto, 18 (background); M. Unal Ozmen/Shutterstock Images, 18 (top left); gerenme/iStockphoto, 18 (top middle); Lana B/Shutterstock Images, 18 (top right); alarich/iStockphoto, 18 (bottom left); mishu/Shutterstock Images, 18 (bottom middle); schab/Shutterstock Images, 18 (bottom right); AP Images, 21, 27; Jacob A. Riis/Museum of the City of New York/Archive Photos/Getty Images, 22–23; Corbis Historical/Getty Images, 25; Everett Historical/Shutterstock Images, 31, 33, 36–37; Red Line Editorial, 39

ISBN
978-1-63517-878-4 (hardcover)
978-1-63517-979-8 (paperback)
978-1-64185-182-4 (ebook pdf)
978-1-64185-081-0 (hosted ebook)

Library of Congress Control Number: 2018931682

Printed in the United States of America
Mankato, MN
May, 2018

ABOUT THE AUTHOR

Rachel Hamby grew up in Utah. She wasn't a pioneer, but her great-great-grandpa came to the West in the mid-1800s. In 1887, he received an award for producing the first 7,000 pounds of sugar sold in Utah. Isn't that sweet?

R0453301475

TABLE OF CONTENTS

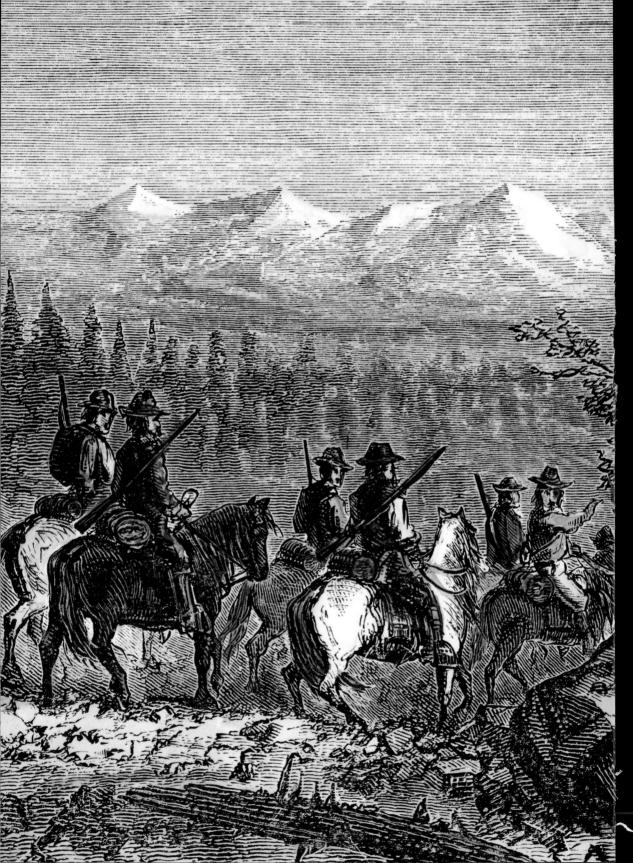

CHAPTER 1

WESTWARD EXPANSION

When the United States declared its independence in 1776, the new nation was made up of 13 states. However, many US leaders wanted the country to expand westward. In 1803, the nation doubled in size due to the Louisiana Purchase. This vast territory stretched from the Mississippi River to the Rocky Mountains.

In 1846, the United States gained the Oregon Territory. This piece of land was in the Northwest.

A group of riders get their first view of the Sierra Nevada range as they head west in the 1800s.

▲ Settlers built new towns in the western territories.

It stretched to the Pacific Ocean. After winning the Mexican–American War (1846–1848), the United States also gained a huge piece of land in the Southwest. These western regions became known as the American frontier.

Families traveled to the American frontier with hopes of a better life. Farmers made the journey for fertile land. **Prospectors** went in search of silver and gold. Black people sought freedom and safety after the US Civil War (1861–1865).

However, traveling to the frontier wasn't easy. Some families made the journey over difficult terrain. Others sailed around the southern tip of South America. **Immigrants** sailed across oceans.

American Indian and Hispanic families already lived in the West when US settlers arrived. Large numbers of settlers forced these groups of people off their homelands. In the process, they threatened the cultural traditions of the American Indian and Hispanic peoples.

Westward expansion was a time of massive change in the United States. And children were there to experience it all.

THINK ABOUT IT ◁

The journey to the West was long and dangerous. Why do you think people risked their lives to move there?

CHAPTER 2

THE FIRST CHILDREN OF THE WEST

American Indians lived in North America for more than 10,000 years before the first Europeans arrived. They were **descendants** of people who crossed into North America from Asia. These ancient travelers journeyed across a land bridge from northeast Asia to Alaska. They formed tribes and nations throughout the North American continent.

Many American Indian tribes used cradleboards to carry babies. Some still use cradleboards today.

Some American Indian children lived in different locations throughout the year. Their tribes moved between summer and winter camps. They followed herds of buffalo and antelope. American Indians hunted these animals for food and made clothing from their hides.

Jumping Badger was born in 1831. His tribe lived near the Grand River in present-day South Dakota. He was a member of the Hunkpapa Lakota Sioux tribe. In summer, Jumping Badger followed buffalo across the country's grassy plains. By the age of 10, he was hunting with his tribe. In winter, his family took shelter in valleys. They built a fire in the center of their tipi to stay warm. Jumping Badger ate buffalo meat that he cooked on the fire. At night, he slept on a thick buffalo hide.

When Jumping Badger was 14, he fought in a battle with a **rival** tribe. Afterward, his father

△ Sitting Bull led the Lakota Sioux through years of resistance to the US government.

changed Jumping Badger's name to Sitting Bull. He was impressed with his son's strength and bravery. Sitting Bull fought in many battles to protect the land his tribe called home. He fought other tribes in some battles and US troops in others. In 1869, Sitting Bull became chief of the Lakota Sioux nation.

▲ Grass homes consisted of wooden frames and long prairie grass.

Maria Chona grew up in the desert in the 1850s. Her tribe, the Tohono O'odham, lived in present-day Arizona. Maria lived in a round grass home. But she spent most of her time outdoors.

Maria woke up early each morning and ran with the other girls to the hills. They gathered red, muddy water in jars. Then they packed the jars in nets, placing sticks in between the jars so they wouldn't break. The older girls strapped the nets to their backs and ran all the way home. Running was an important part of Tohono life. Children ran long distances to stay healthy and strong. At night, Maria crawled through the small door of her home. She fell asleep on a mat of woven cactus fibers.

As she grew, Maria saw the life of the Tohono people change. In 1916, the US government relocated the Tohono O'odham tribe to a **reservation**. The government wanted American Indians to **assimilate** into European-American society. But the Tohono people fought to preserve their traditions. Many of these traditions are still practiced today.

THINK ABOUT IT ◄

American Indian nations lived out their own cultures for centuries. Why do you think the US government wanted to change their ways of life?

ZITKALA-SA

Zitkala-Sa was born in South Dakota in 1876. Her mother was a Yankton Sioux, and her father was European-American. When Zitkala-Sa was eight years old, her mother sent her away to school.

At the time, **missionaries** convinced many American Indian parents to send their children to **boarding schools**. Other American Indian children were forced into the schools. These schools prohibited American Indian children from practicing their cultures. The children weren't allowed to speak their native languages. They were forced to adopt European-American culture.

On the day of her departure, Zitkala-Sa stood with her friends, who were also leaving. "Soon we were being drawn rapidly away by the white man's horses," Zitkala-Sa later wrote. "When I saw the lonely figure of my mother vanish in the distance, a sense of regret settled heavily upon me."

Girls learn cooking skills at an American Indian boarding school in Pennsylvania in 1903.

The train ride to Wabash, Indiana, took several days. "It was night when we reached the school grounds," Zitkala-Sa recalled. "My body trembled more from fear than from the snow I trod upon."

At school, the adults cut off Zitkala-Sa's long hair and taught her about the Bible. Zitkala-Sa longed for her old life. She often felt torn between her native culture and the pressure to assimilate. When she grew up, Zitkala-Sa stood up for American Indians as a writer and activist.

Zitkala-Sa. *American Indian Stories, Legends, and Other Writings*. New York: Penguin Books, 2003. Print. 86, 88.

CHAPTER 3

AN OVERLAND JOURNEY

Some of the first white settlers in the West were **pioneer** families looking to start new lives in the Oregon Territory. Many traveled west on the Oregon Trail. Starting from Missouri, the 2,000-mile (3,200-km) journey took four to five months. The pioneers, including children, walked 15 miles (24 km) per day. They crossed prairies, deserts, and mountains. The children often walked barefoot, since their shoes caused blisters.

A pioneer couple stops for lunch while traveling through Kansas.

In 1845, seven-year-old Benjamin Bonney lived with his family in Smithfield, Illinois. That year, his family decided to move to the Oregon Territory. To prepare for the trip, Benjamin's father built a prairie schooner. This wagon had a wooden base and a canvas top to protect the family's belongings from dust, sun, and rain.

➤ PACKING THE PRAIRIE SCHOONER

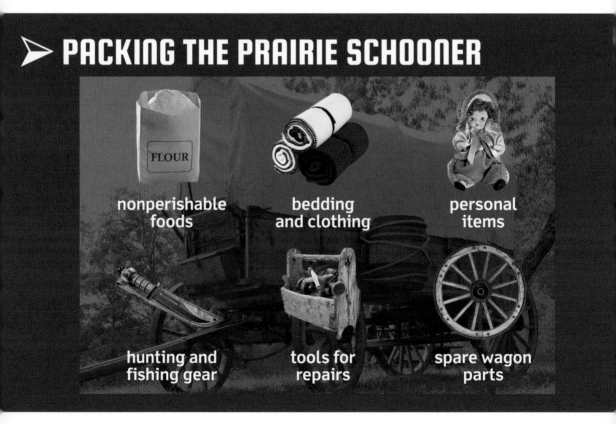

nonperishable foods

bedding and clothing

personal items

hunting and fishing gear

tools for repairs

spare wagon parts

Prairie schooners were rarely used for riding. Their wooden wheels bounced heavily along rocky trails. This made it uncomfortable to ride inside.

Once the wagon was loaded, it was hitched to a team of oxen. Then Benjamin's family started their journey on the trail. They traveled with other families as part of a wagon train. One day, the group stopped at a trading post in Idaho. Trading posts were popular spots to rest and exchange goods. American Indians, fur trappers, and pioneers gathered to trade buffalo meat, hides, dry goods, and weapons.

At the post, a fur trapper convinced some families to change their course. The next morning, Benjamin's father pulled the wagon off the Oregon Trail. They headed for California instead.

Many pioneers feared that American Indians would attack them on their journey to the West.

But Benjamin was interested in the American Indians he met along the way. During his travels, a group of American Indians offered him bread made with crickets and dried acorns. He liked the bread, even though the ingredients surprised him.

Benjamin witnessed horrible violence against American Indians on his trip. One man in his group captured and beat an American Indian man. Benjamin saw another American Indian man being shot and killed. Compared to other dangers, American Indians posed little threat to pioneers. The travelers' most common cause of death was sickness. Diseases such as cholera killed as many as 30,000 pioneers on the Oregon Trail.

When Benjamin's family reached California, they camped near a shallow stream. Benjamin waded in the cool water and spotted a yellow rock. One of the other travelers told Benjamin it was

Miners pan for gold in El Dorado County, California, in 1890.

gold. Four years later, a man working on a sawmill discovered flakes of gold in another California river. This discovery led to the California Gold Rush of 1849. People from around the world traveled to California to mine for gold.

In California, two of Benjamin's siblings died of illness. Afterward, the family decided to return to their original plan. They continued their journey to Oregon on horseback. The family finally arrived in June 1846, more than a year after leaving Illinois.

CHAPTER 4

ORPHANS IN THE WEST

In the 1800s, waves of immigrants entered the United States. Many settled in New York City, causing the area to become overcrowded. Families struggled to find places to live. Food became scarce. Many children lost their parents to disease. Other parents sent their children to orphanages because they couldn't take care of them. However, orphanages were also overcrowded. Thousands of children had no place to go but the streets.

Boys stand with their belongings in New York City in the late 1800s, ready to head west.

In 1853, Charles Loring Brace founded the Children's Aid Society (CAS) in New York City. This organization sent homeless or abused children to families living in the West. Many farming families wanted older children to work on their farms. Other families were looking for children to love and raise as their own. Between 1854 and 1929, CAS sent more than 200,000 children to homes across the country. The children traveled on trains from New York, Boston, and other cities on the East Coast.

> ## ➤ THINK ABOUT IT

Some of the children who rode orphan trains left behind family members in New York City. Their families wanted them to have better lives. How might it have felt for these children to leave home?

The Children's Aid Society ran lodging houses and schools in New York City for homeless children.

Irma Craig was three years old when she left New York on an orphan train in 1901. CAS agents had sewn a large card with the number 32 onto Irma's jacket. When the train arrived in Missouri, Irma rushed to meet the woman taking her in.

Katherine Boehm was waiting at the station, holding a card with the number 32 on it.

Katherine and her husband, George Boehm, had two foster sons. However, Katherine also wanted a daughter. Irma built a strong bond with her adopted mother. Irma's foster brothers were older than she was, so she played with the cats, dogs, and ducks on the farm. When Irma started school, she met other children who had come to Missouri on orphan trains. These children became Irma's close friends.

When Irma was around 10 years old, her foster mother died of an illness. Her foster father did not know how to help Irma or take away her sadness. He thought Irma might be happier in a home with a mother, so he asked neighbors to take her in. Irma moved in with Adelheid Gnagi, who lived with her brother and her 18-year-old daughter.

The expansion of railroads in the 1860s allowed more children to move to the West.

Irma went on to become a teacher, wife, and the mother to eight children. She shared the stories of her youth with her children, who were amazed at all she had overcome.

Many orphan train riders suffered great hardship. Some were separated from brothers or sisters. Others were used strictly as farm labor or treated with abuse and neglect. However, many children that rode the orphan trains lived good lives on the frontier. They escaped a life of poverty on the city streets.

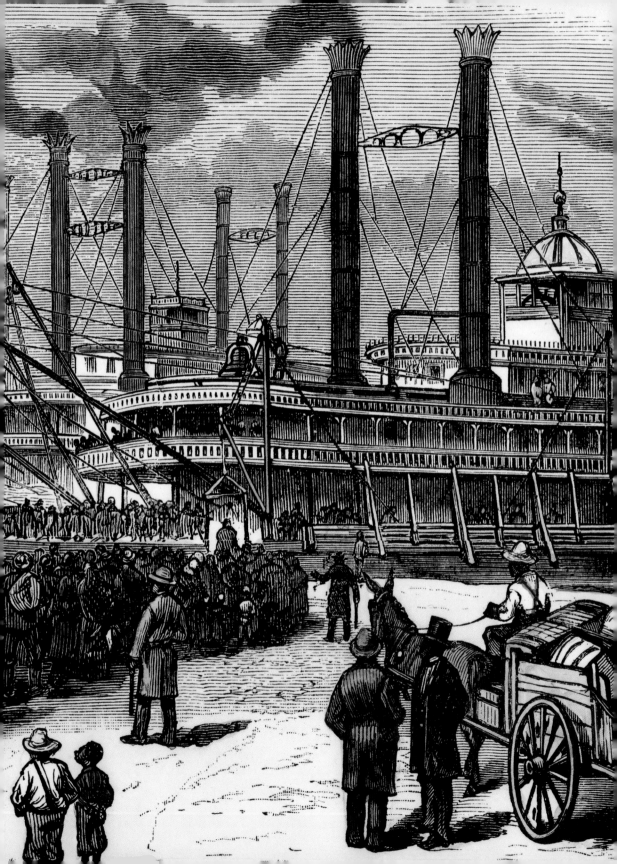

CHAPTER 5

SETTLING ON A HOMESTEAD

In 1862, US President Abraham Lincoln signed the Homestead Act. Under this act, settlers could purchase up to 160 acres of public land in the West for $1.25 per acre. They could also gain ownership of the land by living on it for five years. The act gave many struggling families the opportunity to build new lives.

The Homestead Act came at an important time in US history. The Civil War brought great change.

After the Civil War, large numbers of black people left the South.

In the five years after the end of the war, the US government passed three amendments to the US Constitution. The Thirteenth Amendment banned slavery, freeing more than four million enslaved people. The Fourteenth and Fifteenth Amendments gave black people full citizenship and the right to vote. However, white leaders in numerous states passed laws that restricted black people's freedom. Many white people treated black people with prejudice, racism, and violence.

Under the Homestead Act, all US citizens could apply for a parcel of land. This included women, black people, and immigrants. The opportunity to own land and build a homestead drew thousands of black people to the West.

In 1877, Emma Williams boarded a train in Lexington, Kentucky. Her husband and parents traveled by her side. Emma was eight months

🔺 This family settled on a homestead in Nicodemus, Kansas, in the late 1800s.

pregnant, and she hoped for a better future for herself and her child. She was one of the many black people heading to the frontier. These determined individuals who traveled by boat, rail, and foot to Kansas became known as Exodusters.

Emma and her family got off the train in Ellis, Kansas. They still had a 35-mile (56-km) journey ahead of them. From Ellis, they walked for two days before reaching Nicodemus, Kansas.

Nicodemus was founded in 1877 by a group of freed slaves from Kentucky. Emma was one of the first 300 settlers to arrive. When she had her little boy, Henry, he became the first freeborn child in Nicodemus.

Henry grew up on his family's homestead with his parents and grandparents. His mother and father had five more children. The large family lived in a dugout, a common home in pioneer times. Because few trees grew on the Kansas prairie, pioneers couldn't build wood houses. Instead, they dug their homes from the sides of hills. Dugout homes looked similar to caves.

In 1879, two settlers created the first school in Nicodemus. Jenny Smith Fletcher and her husband, Zachary, taught lessons to 15 children. They taught these lessons in a dugout until Zachary built a building a few years later. The

▲ By 1880, settlers had established several buildings, including churches and stores, in Nicodemus.

settlers of Nicodemus used the building as a school, post office, and hotel.

Exodusters established their freedom and independence by founding settlements in the West. The settlers in these towns still experienced discrimination and prejudice. But by moving to the West, they had found greater opportunities to build new lives.

MOLLIE SHEEHAN

In 1865, 12-year-old Mollie Sheehan lived with her family in Montana. She had been born in Louisville, Kentucky. But after her mother died and her father remarried, her family moved to the West. Most of Mollie's friends were from the South. Their families had all moved to the frontier during the Civil War. Many held harsh views against people from the North, including President Abraham Lincoln.

That April, Lincoln was assassinated. The news came to Montana through the Pony Express. This company hired relay riders to deliver mail across the country on horseback. Later, Mollie wrote about the way her friends reacted to the news: "The Southern girls . . . picked up their ankle-length skirts to their knees and jigged and hippity-hopped around and around the room. . . . They believed [Lincoln was] the first and last

A Pony Express rider arrives at a station in the Rocky Mountains.

cause of any and every misfortune that had befallen their parents."

Mollie's friends encouraged her to dance with them. Mollie remembered their words: "Come on, Mollie, come on join the dance; you're from Kentucky; you're a Southerner!" Mollie joined her friends, but she felt guilty. "They had reawakened in me all the prejudices that were mine because of my Kentucky birth," she wrote. Years later, Mollie still felt ashamed of how she acted that day.

Mary Ronan and Margaret Ronan. *Girl from the Gulches: The Story of Mary Ronan*. Helena, MT: Montana Historical Society, 2003. Print. 47–48.

CHAPTER 6

WORK AND PLAY

Children worked hard on the frontier. Many families lived on farms, where there was always plenty that needed to be done. Children collected eggs, herded sheep, and milked cows. In the fields, they picked weeds and chased away crows.

Hunting was an important part of life for families in the West. Children as young as seven or eight years old helped hunt animals for food.

A pioneer family keeps busy with chores and games outside their cabin.

Lee Whipple-Haslam was only 11 years old when her father died. After that, Lee took on all the hunting for her family. Her mother was busy running their boarding house. The animals Lee hunted provided food for all the boarders.

Children on the frontier often found jobs outside their homes. In Montana, Mollie Sheehan picked flowers for hotels. She earned 25 cents' worth of gold dust for each bundle she sold.

Teenage boys sometimes worked for the Pony Express. However, Pony Express riders needed riding experience. The job required them to ride long distances at top speeds. Most riders weighed less than 125 pounds (57 kg). This helped the horses move faster.

Children easily found jobs in boom towns. These were towns that experienced rapid and sudden growth, often due to mining. Children in boom towns sold newspapers, matchsticks, fruit, and fish. Boys often worked for mines, separating coal from stone. Children of **migrants** harvested crops with their parents. Some child workers helped support their families instead of going to school.

THE PONY EXPRESS (1860-1861) ◄

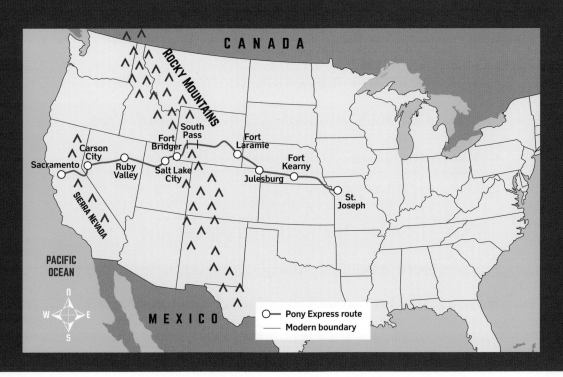

Many parents wanted their children to receive an education, but resources were scarce. In the early days of the frontier, children did schoolwork at home. Parents taught their children how to spell and read in the evenings. As settlers established towns, parents and community leaders organized schools. They hired teachers who traveled by train to the West. Children of all ages attended class in one-room schoolhouses.

Work and school kept children busy. But families somehow made time for play. Children played with dolls, juggled stones, and spun tops made from acorns. They also wrestled and ran races with their friends.

Many frontier children loved ponies and horses. Horses were a part of nearly every culture on the frontier. For instance, Lorin Brown grew up in the southwestern town of Taos, New Mexico. Lorin

A Children sit by a stream near Taos, New Mexico, in 1905. In the West, children spent most of their time outdoors.

and his friends would pretend they were horses. In central Montana, Kaia Lien harnessed a wild horse with the strings from her **petticoat**. When she brought the horse home, her mother told her to put it back where she found it.

In the West, children had to put in a hard day's work. Parents needed their children to lend a helping hand. This was how families survived. Fortunately, hard work was often followed by playtime, games, or a family picnic.

CHAPTER 7

CHANGES IN THE WEST

In 1869, US railway companies completed the Transcontinental Railroad. Now families could go west by train. The Transcontinental Railroad changed how Americans lived. Trains could move goods from coast to coast. This made items such as sewing machines, farm equipment, and other supplies cheaper and easier to attain. Trains could also transport construction materials. Western cities grew quickly along the railroad.

Approximately 15,000 workers helped build the Transcontinental Railroad.

In 1912, the US government created the Children's Bureau. This government office focused on the well-being of children and mothers. Later, in 1938, the US government passed the Fair Labor Standards Act. This act prohibited children from working dangerous jobs outside the home. In addition, children younger than 16 could not work during school hours.

Advances in health and medicine also improved children's lives. By 1900, 40 states had health departments that created standards for water treatment and food safety. This prevented the spread of many diseases. The number of doctors also rose, and doctors received better training.

Progress on the frontier often came at terrible costs. The US government had forced American Indians off their sacred lands. Other tribes saw the boundaries of their lands shrink. American

▲ Children on the American frontier helped their families survive.

Indian, Hispanic, and black children faced prejudice and discrimination. As white settlers pressured children to assimilate, entire cultures were erased.

The children on the American frontier lived varied and diverse lives. They forged new communities on a land that changed and grew with them. The history of the West reflects these children's strength, struggle, and hard work.

FOCUS ON
CHILDREN ON THE AMERICAN FRONTIER

Write your answers on a separate piece of paper.

1. Write a paragraph that summarizes the main ideas of Chapter 5.

2. Do you think the orphan trains were a good solution for homeless children on the East Coast? Why or why not?

3. Which amendment to the US Constitution banned slavery?

      A. the Thirteenth Amendment
      B. the Fourteenth Amendment
      C. the Fifteenth Amendment

4. Why did the Homestead Act motivate Americans to move to the frontier?

      A. It made land more expensive in the East.
      B. It offered cheap land in the West.
      C. It paid for travelers' food and supplies.

Answer key on page 48.

GLOSSARY

assimilate
To become part of a group, culture, or society.

boarding schools
Schools where students live and study.

descendants
People who come from a particular family, ancestor, or group of people.

immigrants
People who move to a new country.

migrants
Workers who move from place to place to do seasonal work.

missionaries
People who teach religious beliefs and attempt to convince others of those beliefs.

petticoat
A gathered skirt worn under a dress.

pioneer
Among the first to settle in a new land.

prospectors
People who search for valuable materials such as gold or oil.

reservation
An area of land set aside for American Indian people.

rival
In competition with another person or group of people.

TO LEARN MORE

BOOKS

Langston-George, Rebecca. *Orphan Trains.* North Mankato, MN: Capstone Press, 2016.

Sandler, Martin W. *Iron Rails, Iron Men, and the Race to Link the Nation.* Somerville, MA: Candlewick Press, 2015.

Stuckey, Rachel. *African Americans in the West.* New York: PowerKids Press, 2016.

NOTE TO EDUCATORS

Visit **www.focusreaders.com** to find lesson plans, activities, links, and other resources related to this title.

INDEX

Answer Key: 1. Answers will vary; **2.** Answers will vary; **3.** A; **4.** B